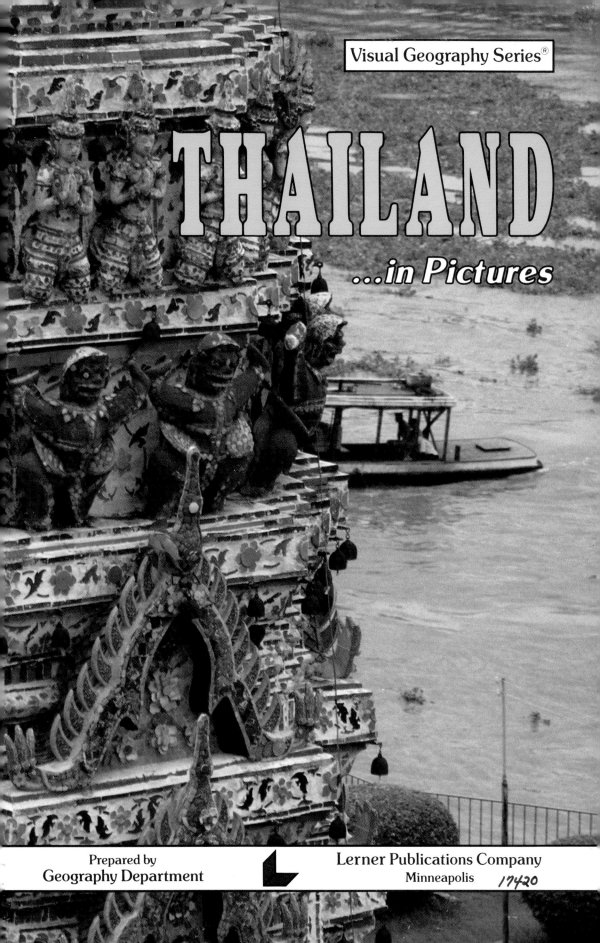

Visual Geography Series®

THAILAND
...in Pictures

Prepared by
Geography Department

Lerner Publications Company
Minneapolis

17420

Independent Picture Service

A monk delivers a religious sermon in the presence of several faithful Buddhists.

This is an all-new edition of the Visual Geography Series. Previous editions have been published by Sterling Publishing Company, New York City, and some of the original textual information has been retained. New photographs, maps, charts, captions, and updated information have been added. The text has been entirely reset in 10/12 Century Textbook.

LIBRARY OF CONGRESS CATALOGING-IN-PUBLICATION DATA

Thailand in pictures / prepared by Geography
  Department, Lerner Publications Company.

    p. cm. — (Visual geography series)
    Rev. ed. of: Thailand in pictures / prepared by James
Nach.
    Includes index.
    Summary: An introduction to the history, land, people, government, economy, and culture of the southeast Asian country once known as Siam.
    ISBN 0-8225-1866-X (lib. bdg.)
    1. Thailand. [1. Thailand.] I. Nach, James. Thailand in pictures. II. Lerner Publications Company. Geography Dept. III. Series: Visual geography series (Minneapolis, Minn.)
DS563.5.T4577   1989   88-37906
959.3-dc19   CIP
                                        AC

International Standard Book Number: 0-8225-1866-X
Library of Congress Catalog Card Number: 88-37906

VISUAL GEOGRAPHY SERIES®

Publisher
Harry Jonas Lerner
Associate Publisher
Nancy M. Campbell
Senior Editor
Mary M. Rodgers
Editors
Gretchen Bratvold
Dan Filbin
Photo Researcher
Karen A. Sirvaitis
Editorial/Photo Assistant
Marybeth Campbell
Consultants/Contributors
Montree Socatiyanurak
Sandra K. Davis
Designer
Jim Simondet
Cartographer
Carol F. Barrett
Indexers
Kristine S. Schubert
Sylvia Timian
Production Manager
Gary J. Hansen

Independent Picture Service

In northern Thailand, an elderly Thai fishes from a riverbank.

Acknowledgments

Title page photo by Drs. A. A. M. van der Heyden, Naarden, the Netherlands.

Elevation contours adapted from *The Times Atlas of the World*, seventh comprehensive edition (New York: Times Books, 1985).

1 2 3 4 5 6 7 8 9 10 98 97 96 95 94 93 92 91 90 89

Schoolchildren climb a jungle gym at a playground in Bangkok, Thailand's capital city. The spire in the background rises from a *chedi*, a sacred building and symbol of Buddhism – Thailand's main religion.

Contents

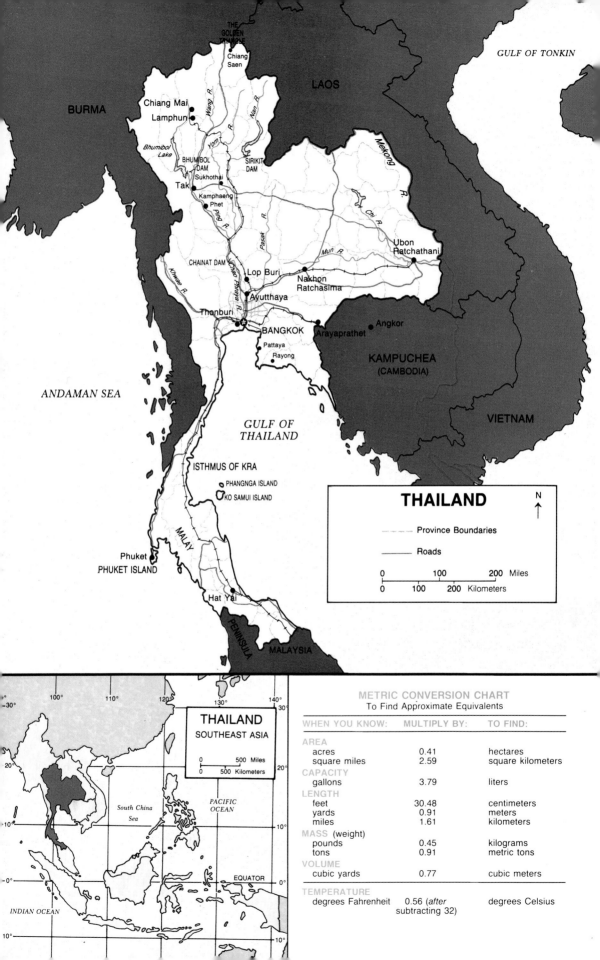

THAILAND

- – · – Province Boundaries
- ——— Roads

| 0 | 100 | 200 Miles |
| 0 | 100 | 200 | Kilometers |

N

THE GOLDEN TRIANGLE
Chiang Saen
BURMA
Chiang Mai
Lamphun
LAOS
GULF OF TONKIN
Wang R.
Yom R.
Nan R.
Bhumibol Lake
BHUMIBOL DAM
SIRIKIT DAM
Mekong R.
Tak
Sukhothai
Kamphaeng Phet
Ping R.
Pasak R.
Chi R.
Ubon Ratchathani
Mun R.
CHAINAT DAM
Lop Buri
Nakhon Ratchasima
Khwae R.
Chao Phraya
Ayutthaya
Thonburi
BANGKOK
Arayaprathet
Angkor
KAMPUCHEA (CAMBODIA)
Pattaya
Rayong
VIETNAM
ANDAMAN SEA
GULF OF THAILAND
ISTHMUS OF KRA
PHANGNGA ISLAND
KO SAMUI ISLAND
MALAY
Phuket
PHUKET ISLAND
Hat Yai
PENINSULA
MALAYSIA

THAILAND
SOUTHEAST ASIA

| 0 | 500 Miles |
| 0 | 500 Kilometers |

-30°
100°
110°
120°
130°
140°
30°
20°
PACIFIC OCEAN
South China Sea
20°
10°
10°
EQUATOR
0°
INDIAN OCEAN
10°
10°

The galleries of Wat Benchamabopitr in Bangkok contain a valuable collection of statues of Buddha—the "Enlightened One" who is honored as the founder of Buddhism. Influenced at first by artists from India, Kampuchea, and China, Thai craftspeople gradually developed their own style of Buddhist art.

Photo by Josh Kohnstamm

Introduction

Thailand, a nation in Southeast Asia, has a long history of independence. In the Thai language, the country's official name is Muang Thai, meaning "land of the free." Even when European powers colonized parts of Asia between the sixteenth and nineteenth centuries, Thai kings managed to avoid foreign domination. While maintaining their independence, the Thai adopted some of the ideas that Western nations brought to Southeast Asia.

Many cultures have contributed to the Thai way of life. People from India, China, and the island of Sri Lanka—as well as from nearby Southeast Asian territories—have traded and settled in Thailand. Their religions, social systems, and technologies have helped to shape the country.

Throughout much of its history, Thailand has had able and progressive kings. Since 1932, however, a constitutional form of government has greatly reduced the monarch's power. Under the new system, the nation's leaders have changed frequently, and the country has had little political stability.

Although its political leadership since the 1930s has not been consistent or enduring, Thailand has made steady economic progress. Huge rice crops from central Thailand have fed the Thai people and have provided the nation with a strong agricultural economy. Expanded industries have also helped the economy to grow, and Thailand looks forward to increasing prosperity in the twenty-first century.

Farmers use water buffalo and wooden plows to cultivate rice on the fertile central plain. Rice was Thailand's main export until the late 1970s, when cassava (a root crop) became a leading agricultural export.

1) The Land

Thailand occupies nearly 200,000 square miles of territory in the center of Southeast Asia, making the country almost as large as the states of Colorado and Nevada combined. Thailand includes a narrow strip that juts southward along a 550-mile-long portion of the Malay Peninsula, which Thailand shares with Burma and Malaysia.

Thailand's border with Burma extends beyond the peninsula to the west and northwest. Laos and Kampuchea (also known as Cambodia) lie along the nation's eastern boundary. The Gulf of Thailand, an arm of the South China Sea, forms the country's southern edge. The Andaman Sea—a part of the Indian Ocean—stretches along the western coast of peninsular Thailand.

Several islands lie off the shores of Thailand. Phuket is the largest Thai island in the Andaman Sea, and Ko Samui is one of the larger islands in the Gulf of Thailand. Many Thai islands contain untapped mineral resources. They also have potential for tourism because of their fine, unspoiled beaches.

Topography

Thailand extends for almost 1,100 miles from north to south, and it is about 500 miles across at its widest point. The nation's territory falls into four topographical regions—the central plain, the Khorat Plateau, the northern mountains, and the southern peninsula.

THE CENTRAL PLAIN

The most populous region in the country is the central plain, which extends almost 300 miles northward from the Gulf of Thailand to the foothills of the northern mountains. The Bilauktaung Mountains form the plain's western boundary, and the Phetchabun Mountains define part of the region's eastern edge.

The terrain of the central plain is very flat, and a large river system—the Chao Phraya and its tributaries—dominates the landscape. This waterway irrigates the soil, making the plain a fertile agricultural area that yields large harvests of rice. An extensive network of canals—called *klongs* —provides additional irrigation and access to river traffic.

THE KHORAT PLATEAU

The square-shaped Khorat Plateau is located in northeastern Thailand at an average elevation of 1,000 feet above sea level. The Phetchabun Mountains border the plateau on the west, and the Phanom Dong Rak range marks the plateau's southern boundary. The Mekong River flows along the northern and eastern limits of the plateau.

Composing about one-third of the nation's land area, the Khorat Plateau is the least fertile area of the country. The sandy soil and seasonal droughts and rains make farming difficult. Nevertheless, Thai farmers grow rice in the areas of the plateau that can be irrigated.

Small boats glide on the Chao Phraya River. The river, along with its tributaries and *klongs* (canals), forms the central plain's waterway network. The Chao Phraya—whose name means "mother of noble waters" in the Thai language—empties into the Gulf of Thailand.

Photo by Andrew E. Beswick

THE NORTHERN MOUNTAINS

The northern mountain ranges, which run in a north-south direction, compose about one-fourth of the nation's territory. These peaks lie along Thailand's borders with Burma to the west and Laos to the northeast. Elevations are the highest in the west, and the tallest point in the country, Doi Inthanon (8,587 feet), stands in the extreme northwestern part of the nation.

Rivers flow between the mountains, and farmers raise crops in the steep river valleys. The rivers wash away sand and mud from the mountainsides and eventually deposit the fertile soil in the central plain. The mountains are heavily forested with evergreens and teak trees, which loggers cut down and float through the rivers to the Gulf of Thailand for processing and export.

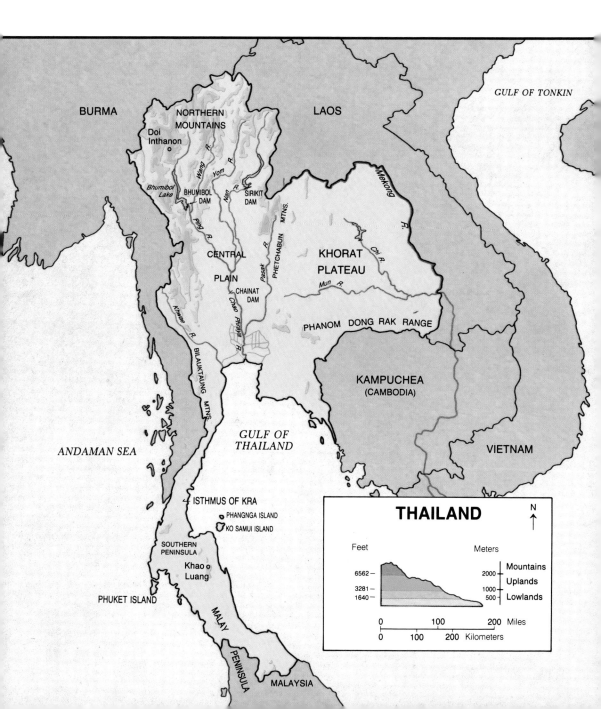

Photo by Mirjam van der Heyden and Charlie Rabelink

The hills of northern Thailand are not easily accessible from the central plain. The sparse population of the highlands includes many small settlements of hill peoples whose ethnic heritage is non-Thai.

THE SOUTHERN PENINSULA

Part of the Malay Peninsula, Thailand's southern peninsular region contains a portion of the Bilauktaung Mountains. The highest point in the peninsular section of this chain is Doi Luang (7,317 feet). The southern peninsula has narrow coastal plains, where farmers cultivate rice, rubber trees, and coconuts.

The section of the peninsula that the Thai and Burmese share varies from 30 to 150 miles in width. The narrowest point is along the Isthmus of Kra. Thai engineers and government leaders have often considered building a canal for shipping across the isthmus (a narrow strip of land that links two larger land areas).

Rivers

Thailand's main river is the Chao Phraya. Flowing southward through the central plain, it provides ample water for the region's many rice fields. The klongs that

Courtesy of Robert E. Olson

In southern Thailand near the Isthmus of Kra, a limestone cave forms a passageway on Phangnga—an island in the Gulf of Thailand.

Photo by Daniel H. Condit

The Ping River flows through Tak, a small city between Bangkok and the city of Chiang Mai.

were built to carry water to the fields also serve as a transportation system and provide a fishing ground for the large population that lives in the area.

Four rivers—the Ping, Wang, Yom, and Nan—are tributaries that begin in the northern mountains and feed the Chao Phraya. The Pasak, which runs parallel to

Courtesy of United Nations

Funded with loans from the World Bank, the Chainat Dam was built in the 1950s to help control flooding by the Chao Phraya River.

Photo by Amandus Schneider

Bangkok, with more than 5.5 million people, is the economic and political hub of Thailand. The Chao Phraya River flows past its modern buildings and ancient temples.

the Phetchabun Mountains in the center of the country, also links up with the Chao Phraya River. Bangkok, Thailand's capital city, lies on the Chao Phraya 20 miles upstream from the Gulf of Thailand.

The Chi and Mun rivers form the main drainage system on the Khorat Plateau. These waterways run eastward into the Mekong River, which winds through Laos, Kampuchea, and Vietnam before going

The broad Mekong River separates Thailand from Laos. The tenth largest waterway in the world, the Mekong defines Thailand's northern and eastern boundaries for 500 miles.

Independent Picture Service

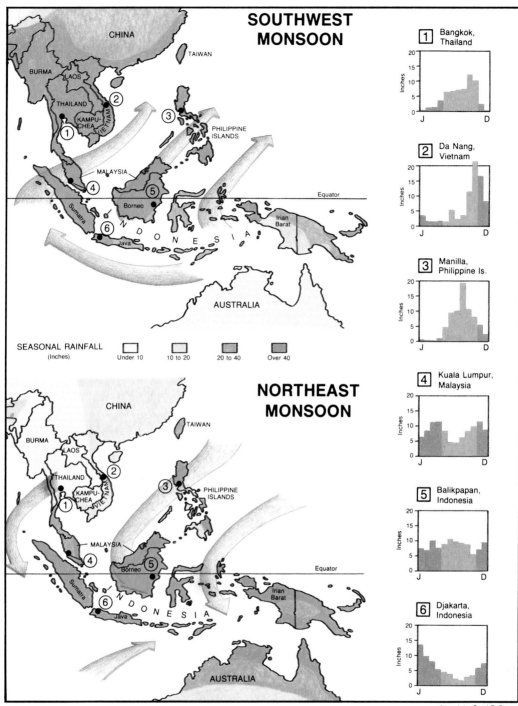

SOUTHWEST MONSOON

NORTHEAST MONSOON

SEASONAL RAINFALL
(Inches)

Under 10   10 to 20   20 to 40   Over 40

1 Bangkok, Thailand

2 Da Nang, Vietnam

3 Manilla, Philippine Is.

4 Kuala Lumpur, Malaysia

5 Balikpapan, Indonesia

6 Djakarta, Indonesia

Artwork by Carol F. Barrett

These maps show the seasonal shift of winds, called monsoons, over Southeast Asia and the rainfall levels for six cities in the region. From May to October, the winds blow from the southwest. From November to April, they come from the northeast. Because the monsoons in Southeast Asia travel over the ocean, they bring rain to coastal and island areas. The southwest monsoon carries rain to Southeast Asia and to islands north of the equator. These areas are dry during the northeast monsoon period. Islands south of the equator receive moisture from the northeast monsoon but are relatively dry during the southwest monsoon period. Both monsoons bring rain to islands on the equator. Bangkok, Thailand, receives most of its rain from May to October, during the southwest monsoon. (Data taken from *World-Climates* by Willy Rudloff, Stuttgart, 1981.)

into the South China Sea. Because of the porous, sandy soil, irrigation is very difficult on the plateau.

Thailand has many short rivers, several small, widely scattered lakes, and a few reservoirs. The plentiful rains that fall during the wet season swell the rivers, providing irrigation for rice and other crops and renewing the nation's water transportation system.

Climate

Monsoons (seasonal winds) determine Thailand's three seasons. In late May a monsoon from the southwest starts to blow over the country, bringing moisture from the Indian Ocean. With the rains comes a hot, wet summer season, which continues until October. Temperatures during this period average 90° F. The southwest monsoon occurs in the summer and carries 90 percent of the country's annual rainfall. About 60 inches of rain fall each year in the northern mountains and in the central plains. The Khorat Plateau receives about 50 inches, and the southern peninsula gets over 100 inches of rainfall annually.

Winds blow from the opposite direction in November, when the northeast monsoon arrives, beginning Thailand's cool, dry winter. The air currents come from continental Asia and blow across the Gulf of Thailand. The monsoon picks up moisture as it crosses the gulf and brings rain to the Malay Peninsula. This moisture accounts for the higher precipitation levels in the southern peninsula, which receives rain during most of the year. The winter air from continental Asia is cool, and temperatures in Thailand range from 50° to 80° F.

The country's hot, dry spring begins in March and lasts until May. Temperatures during this season are usually in the nineties. For example, Bangkok's average temperature during April reaches a very uncomfortable 98° F.

Flora and Fauna

Thailand's vegetation is primarily tropical. The rain-forests of the country's southern peninsula and the coast of the Gulf of Thailand are composed of mangrove, ebony, ironwood, and rattan palm trees. Rain-forests thrive in warm, humid climates, which support the vegetation that grows beneath the forests' tallest trees. Stands of teak, redwood, oak, and evergreen cover the northern mountains. The mountains fringing the Khorat Plateau are also partially covered with evergreen forests.

Over the centuries, people living on the central plain gradually cut down the forests and planted rice fields, which they

Photo by Daniel H. Condit

Lotuses float on the surface of the reservoir formed behind Bhumibol Dam in northern Thailand.

The elephant is considered Thailand's national animal. In northern Thailand, the Center for Training Baby Elephants focuses on breeding elephants, protecting them, and teaching them tasks for the logging industry.

Oxen (above), as well as water buffalo, are used in Thailand for plowing and hauling.

irrigated with water from the Chao Phraya and its tributaries. The Khorat Plateau's vegetation, on the other hand, has changed very little and supports sparse grasses, stunted trees, and thorny shrubs.

Bamboo, a giant variety of grass, grows throughout much of Thailand, especially in the coastal areas. Orchids, gardenias, hibiscus, and many other flowering plants thrive in the country's tropical climate. Fruit trees—such as banana, mango, and coconut—also prosper in Thailand.

Elephants and water buffalo are two of the animal species most useful to the people of Thailand. Asiatic elephants—of which only 15,000 remained in the wild in the mid-1980s—are often trained to move timber from the northern mountain forests to rivers. The logs then float down the waterways to the Gulf of Thailand for export. Farmers frequently use water buffalo to pull plows and to crush grain. In addition to their value as labor animals, water buffalo are cheap to feed because they eat rough fodder that other animals cannot digest.

Tigers, leopards, rhinoceroses, Himalayan black bears, gibbons (tailless apes), and other animals live in the wilderness areas of the nation, especially in reserves such as Doi Inthanon National Park. Perhaps best known of all the Thai animals is the Siamese cat, which was introduced to Western countries in the nineteenth century.

Thailand's rivers and coastal waters host many varieties of fish and seafood, including anchovies, mackerel, shrimp, and crab. Fish also swim in the waters of the flooded rice fields. Crocodiles inhabit the rivers and klongs, and pythons and cobras are two of the many varieties of snakes found in the country. Thailand also has over 800 varieties of birds, including parrots, storks, hornbills, and hawks.

Cities

Although Thailand is predominantly a rural country, people have migrated to the cities at a fast rate since the mid-1960s. Bangkok, known as Krung Thep in the

Photo by Josh Kohnstamm

Hundreds of varieties of birds—including parrots—thrive in Thailand's mild climate.

Courtesy of Tourist Organization of Thailand

The Wat Arun, or Temple of the Dawn, is a striking sight in Bangkok. Its *prangs* (cylindrical towers) symbolize the Buddhist universe. The center prang represents a holy mountain, surrounded by the world's oceans.

As Bangkok has expanded, it has acquired the problems — such as traffic jams — shared by large cities throughout the world.

Wat Phra That Doi Sutep, located near the northern city of Chiang Mai, is one of Thailand's most sacred religious sites. Built in the fourteenth century, the temple attracts thousands of Buddhists, as well as tourists, every year.

16

Thai language, is the nation's capital and largest city, with a population of nearly six million people. Located on the Chao Phraya River, Bangkok is the business, communication, transportation, and political hub of the nation.

Until the 1980s, klongs served as a major means of transportation for many people who lived in the center of the city. In the 1960s, however, some of the klongs began to be filled in to make room for new roads and for new housing. City leaders have not guided the recent development of the urban landscape, and industrial, residential, and commercial buildings stand side by side.

Chiang Mai (population 1.2 million) lies in the Ping River Valley in Thailand's northern mountains. At 1,000 feet above sea level, the city has a cooler climate than most of Thailand. Chiang Mai and the surrounding area contain many historic buildings and temples, such as Wat Phra That Doi Sutep—the region's most important Buddhist religious shrine. The city is also a commercial center for the north, especially for the teak-logging industry. Several ethnic groups from the surrounding mountains sell their handicrafts in the city's markets.

Nakhon Ratchasima (population one million) is an ancient walled town that lies on the Mun River. The site—also known as Khorat—is an important railroad junction and trading center for much of northeastern Thailand. Ubon Ratchathani City (population 800,000), located near the junction of the Chi and Mun rivers, is a commercial hub on the Khorat Plateau.

Hat Yai (population 105,000) is the major trading center on Thailand's southern peninsula. Many Thai, as well as foreign tourists, visit the city while vacationing on the beaches of the southern peninsula.

Photo by Daniel H. Condit

This gate in Nakhon Ratchasima—also called Khorat—was built more than 500 years ago. The largest city in northeastern Thailand, Nakhon Ratchasima is an important transportation center along the Mun River.

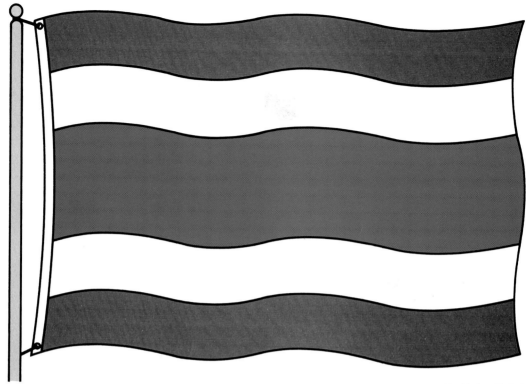

Artwork by Laura Westlund

The central blue stripe of Thailand's flag represents the king and shows the prominent place that royalty holds in the life of the republic. The white stripes stand for Buddhism, and the red bands signify the sacrifice needed to maintain freedom. The flag has been in use since 1917.

2) History and Government

Beginning in the first century A.D., kingdoms whose capitals were outside present-day Thailand dominated the nation's history. In the thirteenth century, realms led by ethnic Thai people developed in central Thailand. These kingdoms controlled the area that would become known as Thailand in the twentieth century.

Many Thai kings were able leaders who kept the territory free from external influences. When European colonizers entered Southeast Asia, Thai rulers maintained their independence either by shutting the Westerners out or by making compromises with them.

Since the 1930s, Thailand's prime ministers—who have come from both military and civilian backgrounds—have struggled to provide political stability. Thailand's history from the 1930s onward has been marked by many attempts to change both the leadership and the governmental structure of the nation.

Prehistory

Distant ancestors of the people of Thailand settled in Southeast Asia about 40,000 years ago. These early Asians defined as their own the territories in which they hunted game animals and gathered edible plants. The groups used bows and arrows, as well as blowpipes and darts, to kill their prey. Archaeologists have found remnants from these early people, including bamboo baskets that were used to carry food and other possessions.

Between 10,000 and 20,000 years ago, people began to farm in the region. Peas, beans, and eventually rice were the main crops that early Southeast Asians grew. Because agriculture provided an opportunity for a more settled way of life, ethnic groups became more distinct from one another.

By the first century A.D., many of these clans had developed small villages and were planting rice as their main food crop. Members of the groups still hunted and gathered food in the forests and fished along the streams of the region. Occasionally, villagers traveled to nearby settlements to trade their surplus goods, which included food, pottery, and metal tools.

Early Kingdoms

The Mon were one of the earliest ethnic groups to become politically organized in the region. In the first century A.D., they established the Funan kingdom, which spread its influence over a large portion of Southeast Asia. At its height, the Funan realm included what are now southern Kampuchea, central Thailand, and the Malay Peninsula.

In the fifth century, Mon merchants established a major commercial center on the Gulf of Thailand to serve ships that traveled between China and India. Contact between Indian traders and the local population brought India's Hindu religion to Southeast Asia. Hindu images and literature played a significant role in the development of Thai culture.

Funan began to decline in the sixth century. Dvaravati, a new Mon kingdom, grew up on the edges of Thailand's central plain. The kingdom drew its economic strength from the overland trade routes that went from Burma, across Thailand, eastward to Kampuchea, and northward to Laos.

At the end of the Funan era, ethnic groups with diverse backgrounds began to move into what is now Thailand. Many of the immigrants came from the Nanchao kingdom, which was located in southern China. Speaking languages collectively referred to as Tai, these people migrated to

A bronze sculpture represents Vishnu, one of the central gods of Hinduism—a religion that came to Thailand from India in about the fifth century A.D.

19

the central and northern areas of Thailand in the seventh century. The Mon referred to the Tai-speakers as Siamese, and these newcomers formed the basis of the modern Thai nation.

Just as they had welcomed Indian culture and the Hindu religion, the Mon were also receptive to monks from the island of Sri Lanka who came to Thailand in the eighth century. These monks were Buddhists, and they taught the Mon the ideas of Gautama Buddha, an Indian religious leader who lived in the sixth century B.C.

Soon after Buddhist monks arrived, Buddhism spread throughout Thailand. Followers of the new faith put up buildings and carved sculptures that they inscribed with words from the Mon language. Despite the possible conflicts between the two faiths, the Buddhist and Hindu cultures were able to exist together harmoniously.

In the tenth century the Khmer Empire, which had its capital at Angkor in Kampuchea, extended its control from the east into Thailand. The Khmer overcame the Mon of the Dvaravati kingdom militarily but did not destroy the Mon's mixed Hindu and Buddhist culture. Instead, Hindu ideas—especially the concept of a divine king—influenced the Khmer, and soon the Khmer king adopted the characteristics of a Hindu god. Throughout their territory,

Photo by Amandus Schneider

Religious shrines—featuring statues of Buddha seated in a pose of meditation—exist throughout the country. Sri Lankan monks first brought the teachings of Buddhism to the region in the eighth century. Thereafter, Buddhist and Hindu influences flourished side by side in Thailand.

By the tenth century, the Khmer Empire extended north into the mountains of modern Thailand and south along the Malay Peninsula. From their capital at Angkor, the Khmer kept in touch with provincial headquarters at Lop Buri, Lamphun, and Chiang Saen.

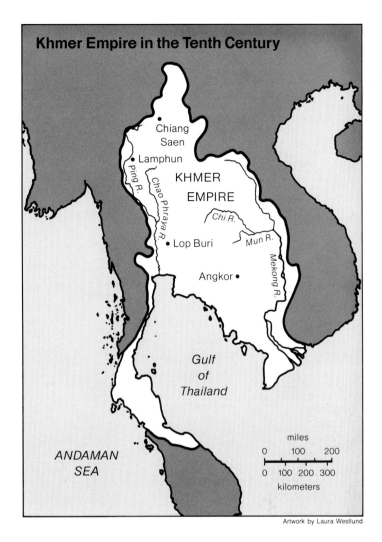

Khmer Empire in the Tenth Century

Chiang Saen

Lamphun

KHMER EMPIRE

Ping R.

Chao Phraya R.

Chi R.

Lop Buri

Mun R.

Angkor

Mekong R.

Gulf of Thailand

ANDAMAN SEA

miles
0   100   200

0   100 200 300
kilometers

Artwork by Laura Westlund

the Khmer built stone palaces and temples in honor of their divine kings.

A system of roads that went from Angkor to provincial urban settlements helped the Khmer to hold their kingdom together. The roads were elevated several feet above the plain to keep them from being flooded during the rainy season.

The Thai Emerge

Although the Khmer initially had authority over them, a new wave of Siamese immigrants gained political and military strength as more of them arrived from southern China. By 1238 they had defeated the Khmer and had set up a Siamese capital at Sukhothai. As they established their first independent kingdom under King Phra Ruang, the Siamese gave themselves the name *Thai*, which means "free people."

The fourth king of Sukhothai, Rama Khamhaeng, began his 40-year reign in 1277. He developed a Thai alphabet that was based on the Khmer writing system and ordered scholars to record his kingdom's history. The king also invited Chinese artisans to Sukhothai, and these craftspeople trained many Thai in the art of making porcelain and pottery. In addition, Rama Khamhaeng encouraged the

21

A group of Buddhist monks and other visitors *(center)* gather among the ruins of Sukhothai—the capital of the Sukhothai kingdom. Coming to power at the end of the thirteenth century, King Rama Khamhaeng extended Sukhothai's political influence. He also encouraged the realm's cultural development.

These fourteenth-century Buddhist religious buildings—called stupas—are part of the ruins of the city of Ayutthaya. In 1350 King Rama Thibodi founded a dynasty (family of rulers) that led Ayutthaya for 400 years.

The Thai built stupas to house artworks or items closely associated with Buddha.

continued spread of Buddhism during his reign.

Under Rama Khamhaeng's stable leadership, Sukhothai expanded its southern and western boundaries and became a more unified empire. The kingdom faltered under the monarchs that followed Rama Khamhaeng, however. By the middle of the fourteenth century, the kingdom of Sukhothai had greatly weakened.

The Kingdom of Ayutthaya

As the Sukhothai Empire declined, many Thai migrated farther south along the Chao Phraya River. By the fourteenth century, several groups inhabited the fertile central plain, where they grew rice and established villages. One of these people, a leader named Rama Thibodi, established a new dynasty (family of rulers) in 1350, with its capital at Ayutthaya. This kingdom overshadowed Sukhothai and had conquered it completely by 1399. Under Rama Thibodi and his successors, the kingdom of Ayutthaya grew to almost the size of present-day Thailand and lasted for over 400 years.

An admirer of Hinduism, Rama Thibodi increased the religion's influence on the people of his kingdom. Although he preserved many Thai legal customs, the king established a system of laws based on the Hindu belief in the unchanging law of nature.

Among the elements in Rama Thibodi's judicial code were rules for giving evidence in a dispute and descriptions of punishments. These laws were the first stage in the development of a detailed pattern of relationships in Thai society. He clearly defined the roles of royalty and subjects, of men and women, and of slaves and free people. A crime by a wealthy person against a farmer, for example, was punished less severely than the same crime committed by a farmer against a member of the rich class.

Despite the king's fondness for Hindu culture and ethics, Buddhism became the dominant religion of the kingdom. Another group of Buddhist monks from Sri Lanka came to the kingdom, and Rama Thibodi allowed Buddhist religious leaders to establish monasteries and temples throughout the region.

While the kingdom developed internally, soldiers from Ayutthaya fought many battles with neighboring Khmer, Burmese, and Malays, as well as with other Thai not under their control. In the late fourteenth and early fifteenth centuries, the kings of Ayutthaya focused particularly on disputes with the Khmer from Angkor. Thai soldiers captured many Khmer prisoners, and in 1431 Angkor was captured and destroyed. Ayutthaya forces also overcame the Malays on the southern peninsula as well as smaller Thai kingdoms near Chiang Mai.

Developments in Ayutthaya

Once its borders were more secure, the Thai government again turned to internal affairs. King Trailok, who ruled from 1448 to 1488, instituted reforms that centralized the national administration. Previously, semi-independent local princes and governors had ruled many of the provinces of Ayutthaya. Trailok established a central government that was composed of separate civil and military branches. Local leaders were called to Ayutthaya and put in charge of the new governmental departments. They were required to live in the capital where the king could easily oversee their work.

King Trailok also formed a rigid class system called *sakdi na*, which means "field power." All male Thai were given the use of varying amounts of land according to their status. Slaves, craftspeople, and other subjects with little status received 10 acres or less, while successful merchants and nobles were given as much as 4,000 acres. Women were not included in this arrangement. Under Trailok's system, a Thai man could change his rank and gain or lose sakdi na depending on whether he gained the favor or displeasure of the king.

Instead of forcing people to pay taxes, the kingdom of Ayutthaya required its subjects to work for the state each year on public projects. The free labor force built roads, canals, palaces, and temples. In order to fulfill the labor requirement, wealthy citizens hired other people to work in their place. Monks and members of the nobility were not required to fulfill the labor tax.

Prisoners taken as a result of military conquest became slaves and worked as laborers on the farms of those with large amounts of sakdi na. In addition, people who could not pay their debts worked for

Courtesy of National Museum, Bangkok

This painting depicts workers and artisans constructing some of the buildings at Ayutthaya. Rama Thibodi and his successors closely modeled the new city on the plan of the previous capital, Sukhothai.

In 1593 the Thai king Naresuan and a Burmese prince faced each other on the battlefield at Nong Sarai. Mounted on their war elephants and accompanied by their foot soldiers, the two leaders clashed. Naresuan killed the Burmese ruler, and the Thai army pushed the invaders from the region.

the person who loaned them money until the debt was settled. This form of labor, called debt slavery, at one time affected 25 percent of the Thai population.

European Contact

At the beginning of the sixteenth century, European explorers sailed their ships into the waters of Southeast Asia. The Portuguese—the first Europeans to make contact with the Thai—arrived in 1511, during the reign of Rama Thibodi II. After establishing a trading post at Malacca on the Malay Peninsula, the Portuguese sought to make a trade arrangement with the Thai government. The newcomers signed treaties with Thai rulers that allowed the Portuguese to live in Ayutthaya and to exchange goods with the local people. Other European trading nations followed the example of the Portuguese,

and soon Southeast Asia became a major commercial region.

Meanwhile, the leaders of Ayutthaya turned their attention to settling where the boundary line would be drawn with neighboring Burma. Disputes had flared for about 40 years in the mid-sixteenth century. The Burmese briefly captured Ayutthaya in 1569, but the Thai king Naresuan defeated Burma's prince in a battle at Nong Sarai in 1593.

With its border secure, the Thai kingdom was able to improve its potential as a European trading outpost. By the early seventeenth century the Dutch and the British had replaced the Portuguese as the most important European trading powers in Southeast Asia. Local rulers permitted both nations to open commercial stations in Thailand. The Thai sent an ambassador to the Netherlands in 1609, which marked the first visit by a Thai to Europe.

Surrounded by Christian missionaries and members of his court, King Narai observed a lunar eclipse by telescope. The missionaries arrived in Thailand in the seventeenth century to convert the Thai people to the Christian religion. The Thai, however, were more interested in gaining Western knowledge than in adopting the faith of the Europeans.

European merchants soon intruded on the internal affairs of the Thai government. Interested in making large profits, the Europeans tried to shape events in the Thai kingdom for their own benefit. On one occasion, the Dutch sailed their warships into the Gulf to Thailand to display their power. This threat alarmed King Narai, who reigned from 1657 to 1688. By giving more trading influence to France—a newcomer in the commercial network—the king weakened the ability of the Dutch to pressure his realm.

Relations between Thailand and European powers became strained. For example, King Louis XIV of France hoped to convert the Thai to Christianity and sent missionaries to Thailand. The missionaries failed, and their interference sparked anti-European feelings. In 1688—after many maneuvers for power among Thai within the royal palace—a Thai group that opposed European influence took over the kingdom. The new rulers expelled most of the Europeans except for a few Dutch and Portuguese traders. The kingdom closed its ports to the Western world until 1826.

The Bangkok Era

Free of European interference, Thai rulers hoped for a period of calm. Burma, the kingdom's neighbor to the west, had remained largely at peace since its defeat by the Thai in 1593. But the Burmese resumed conflict with Thailand in 1760 when they attacked Ayutthaya.

A memorial statue in Thonburi depicts the victorious military leader Phraya Taksin mounted on his horse. Taksin proved to be a much abler general than king, and in 1782 rebels who were dissatisfied with his corrupt government captured and executed him.

In these initial attacks, however, the Burmese failed to overcome the city. Five years later, the Thai again had to defend themselves from their enemy to the west. After 14 months of war, the Burmese captured Ayutthaya. They destroyed buildings, written records, and works of art and killed or imprisoned thousands of Thai.

The Burmese left only small garrisons of their soldiers to protect conquered Thai territory. Phraya Taksin, a Thai general, led his troops against these Burmese detachments in late 1767, driving them out of the region.

Taksin chose Thonburi, a settlement on the Chao Phraya River, as his capital. After proclaiming himself king, Taksin forced rival Thai groups to come under his control. When Burmese troops attempted to retake Thai territory, Taksin's army turned them away. The king reigned until 1782, when rebel leaders overthrew him.

The rebels called on General Phraya Chakkri to be the new Thai king. Chakkri founded a dynasty that continued into the late 1980s. Each king of this dynasty took the ceremonial name Rama, after one of the principal Indian gods. Chakkri moved the capital from Thonburi to Bangkok, just across the Chao Phraya River. Under his rule, the Thai kingdom became known as Siam and included pieces of territory from present-day Kampuchea, Laos, and Malaysia.

By the nineteenth century, Europeans had colonized most of Southeast Asia and were pressuring Thai rulers to widen trade opportunities in Siam. Europeans sent trade representatives to Thai territory during Chakkri's reign but failed to gain commercial access to the region. Later, in 1826, the Thai kingdom and Great Britain signed trade agreements. In 1833 the United States received permission to do business on the same limited basis as the British. By 1851, when King Mongkut (Rama IV) became Siam's monarch, the Thai realm had responded to the requests of foreign merchants for more open markets.

In the late eighteenth century, Phraya Chakkri became the first king of the Rama dynasty. After moving the capital to Bangkok, he built the Wat Phra Keo. Among the decorations inside the temple are golden murals that depict verses from the *Ramakien*—an ancient Hindu epic poem.

King Mongkut's Reign

Before he became king, Mongkut spent 27 years in a Buddhist monastery. During that time he not only read the scriptures of his religion but, with the help of Christian missionaries, also studied science, English, and Western history. Mongkut saw much that was valuable in Western culture. He recognized, however, the threat that Western colonial nations posed to the independence of his kingdom.

The king moved quickly to protect his country by setting foreign nations against one another through competition. He achieved this goal in part by allowing many Western nations to have commercial opportunities in the kingdom. As a result, the king made it possible for colonizing nations to trade successfully in the kingdom without risking Siam's independence.

In 1855 Mongkut signed a treaty with Britain that broadened Thai trade activity, which had been outlined in the 1826 agreement. The new document gave British merchants the right to buy and sell goods directly, without using Thai go-betweens. In addition, the Thai government reduced the heavy taxes that it had previously placed on imports.

British merchants began marketing Thai rice, teak, and tin in world commercial centers, and the Thai bought British manufactured goods, especially cloth, in exchange. Similar treaties were drawn up with the United States, France, Denmark, Portugal, and Italy.

Mongkut welcomed what he judged to be the positive influences of Western commerce on his country. The king encouraged his subjects to study science and European languages with the Christian missionaries who had accompanied the traders to the kingdom. Mongkut ordered a printing press to be set up in Bangkok, and soon a royal newspaper was published.

Independent Picture Service

In the mid-1800s, King Mongkut and Prince Chulalongkorn posed for a photograph in uniforms that were patterned after those of British naval officers. Mongkut had a keen but cautious appreciation for Western ideas and customs.

King Chulalongkorn's Reforms

When Mongkut died in 1868, his son Chulalongkorn (Rama V) became king, and he continued his father's reformation of the kingdom. Chulalongkorn gradually reduced the number of slaves in order to avoid disrupting labor patterns by changing them too quickly. By 1905 the king had eliminated slavery, and debt slavery had also been phased out.

Chulalongkorn reformed the tax system so that Thai citizens contributed money rather than labor to the government. The king also reorganized the sakdi na system. Instead of gaining control of parcels of land as payment for service, government workers and other laborers received salaries.

Among other reforms, Chulalongkorn tried to start a public education system for children in the kingdom. He sponsored the

After Chulalongkorn *(pictured here with one of his sons)* became king in 1868, he often dressed in the clothes of a nineteenth-century European gentleman. Although Chulalongkorn introduced Thailand to some Western modernizations—such as the telegraph and railroads—he also steadfastly maintained his country's independence.

Slavery and debt slavery (paying off a debt through labor) were common when Chulalongkorn became king. Many enslaved workers gained their freedom under this forward-looking king's rule. In 1905 forced labor practices were completely outlawed.

A richly carved royal barge—made from a single tree and powered by 70 rowers—makes its way on the Chao Phraya River. Although Mongkut and Chulalongkorn brought Western ideas to Thailand, they did not put aside the rich Thai heritage.

This railroad track is an updated version of one sponsored by Chulalongkorn at the beginning of the twentieth century. Recognizing the value of Western ideas and technology, Chulalongkorn planned a railroad system that linked many areas of the country to Bangkok.

Photo by Mirjam van der Heyden and Charlie Rabelink

construction of new roads and a railroad network. The king took steps to curb the use of opium (an addictive drug made from opium poppies)—one of the kingdom's goods that was traded with European nations.

Despite expanded trade practices, Great Britain, and later France, still pressured the kingdom for territory. To prevent colonization by these nations, Chulalongkorn attempted to satisfy them by giving them outlying portions of Thai-controlled land.

In 1893 the Thai kingdom surrendered territory east of the Mekong River (in what is now Laos), as well as the western portion of present-day Kampuchea, to the French. In 1904 and 1907, France took smaller portions of Thai territory on the western side of the Mekong River. Great Britain, which was pressuring the Thai from colonies in Burma and Malaya, gained control of Thai areas on the Malay Peninsula. By partially satisfying the Europeans' desire for land, Chulalongkorn enabled most of the Thai kingdom to remain independent.

The Rise of Nationalism

After he reached the throne in 1910, King Vajiravudh (Rama VI) encouraged a spirit of nationalism among the Thai population. Throughout his 15-year reign, he wrote many articles and spoke frequently about the need for loyalty and devotion to the nation. He also organized the highly visible Wild Tiger Corps, which was a military organization and a patriotic civic group.

During World War I (1914–1918), Siam allied itself with France and Great Britain and declared war against Germany. A small force of Thai soldiers went to Europe and joined the fighting. After the war, France and Britain made new treaties with Thailand and gave the Thai a more favorable trade arrangement.

In 1932 a group of dissatisfied military and civilian leaders carried out a coup d'état (a swift, forceful change of government) against the monarchy. Many of these leaders were impatient with the lack of democracy under a system of government ruled by one person. The economic difficulties that the country faced during the worldwide depression of the 1920s and 1930s also spurred the rebels into action.

The leaders of the coup removed the officials appointed by King Prajadhipok (Rama VII), who had taken over the throne in 1925, and reorganized the government. They established a constitution that took away most of the king's power and gave it to elected legislative representatives. This move made Siam a constitutional monarchy—an arrangement that recognized the king as the symbolic ruler but removed his power to administer the country through royal officials.

The civilian leaders of the coup controlled the government until 1938, when Phibun Songgram, a nationalistic leader from the Thai army, became prime minister. Under Phibun's administration, the name of the

King Prajadhipok's royal flag is emblazoned with a *Garuda*—a winged, humanlike figure with the claws and beak of an eagle. Garudas are the mythological protectors of Thai kings, each of whom had his own royal banner.

Artwork by Laura Westlund

country was changed from Siam to Thailand. Phibun's government also pushed for the return of Thai territory that the French and British had absorbed at the turn of the century. After several minor battles against the French in 1940 and 1941, Thailand reclaimed a portion of its lost lands.

World War II and Its Results

During World War II, the Japanese invaded Thailand on December 8, 1941. They fought Thai troops for several hours before Phibun accepted their demand for free access to Burma and Malaya. Later in the month, Thailand sided with Japan against the Allies (Britain, France, and the United States).

Many Thai opposed Thailand's official pro-Japanese stand, and they began the Free Thai movement, which cooperated with the Allies during the war. Over 50,000 Thai actively resisted the Japanese, and many were killed or captured. As the alliance with the Japanese became more like a foreign occupation, Phibun's government became less and less accepted by the Thai. As a result, Phibun was forced from office in mid-1944.

Photo by Mainicki Newspapers

Japanese troops entered Bangkok on December 9, 1941, to the greetings of the city's Japanese residents. They had prepared the way for the enemy assault of Thailand by providing information to the Japanese military.

The governmental ministers who succeeded Phibun came from the country's civilian leaders. The Free Thai movement became more prominent, and, as the war drew to a close, members of the anti-Japanese group met openly in Bangkok. When the war ended in 1945, the Thai government rejected its previous alliance with Japan.

After the war, peace agreements forced Thailand to give up the territory it had regained from France in 1941. Pridi Phanomyong, who had been a powerful influence among the civilian politicians since the 1930s, became prime minister in 1946. Pridi was popular with the Thai because of his strong anti-Japanese views. His leadership quickly ended, however, when King Ananda Mahidol (Rama VIII) was found dead in his palace. Although reportedly the result of an accidental gunshot wound, the king's death aroused concern about the government's role in royal security. Pridi resigned and left the country.

Ananda's brother, 19-year-old Bhumibol Adulyadej (Rama IX), became king in 1946. (Bhumibol still reigned as monarch in the late 1980s.) Because of Pridi's fall from power, civilian politicians lost most of their approval among the Thai people. In November 1947, Phibun and the military had enough popular support to attempt another coup. After overthrowing the civilian government, the new regime held elections in early 1948 that confirmed Phibun as leader of the country.

Coups and Constitutions

Phibun's government withstood several attempted coups in the late 1940s and the early 1950s. Various political groups urged factions within the military to act against the government, but Phibun's larger group of military supporters was always strong enough to thwart opposition.

Phibun was fiercely anti-Communist during his administration. Thailand refused, for example, to recognize the Communist

Photo by Mirjam van der Heyden and Charlie Rabelink

This railway bridge over the Khwae River in western Thailand replaces one constructed during World War II. In 1942 and 1943, the Japanese used Thai and Allied prisoners of war to build a railroad between Bangkok and Rangoon, Burma. Over 90,000 laborers died during the wartime construction of the railway.

regime that founded the People's Republic of China in 1949. Furthermore, new laws harassed Chinese residents of Thailand, especially those who had immigrated to the country since the beginning of the twentieth century. The Thai government also supported anti-Communist movements in Korea and Vietnam.

Some Thai believed Phibun's government was ineffective. As a result, Field Marshal Sarit Thanarat successfully overthrew Phibun in 1957. Sarit suspended the laws of the land—including voting rights—and called for a new constitution. In the absence of an active constitution, Sarit ruled Thailand under martial (military) law.

Sarit, like Phibun, was strongly anti-Communist, but he also managed the economy well—something Phibun had not done. Under Sarit's leadership, sanitation

A Hindu priest pours purifying water over King Bhumibol's hands as part of his coronation ceremony in May 1950. Most Thai rituals are Buddhist in their origin, but many include Hindu traditions that were adopted by the Thai beginning in the fifteenth century.

Prime Minister Thanom Kittikachorn poses in full military dress during a state occasion in 1964. After governing Thailand from 1963 to 1973, Thanom lost the king's favor when government troops killed university students who were demonstrating for political reform. Without the king's support, the prime minister resigned and fled the country.

improved, and more areas of the country received electricity. The field marshal welcomed foreign investment and sponsored new industries, which led to increased employment. In 1963 Sarit died, and his deputy, General Thanom Kittikachorn, succeeded him.

Thanom gradually restored political rights in Thailand, beginning in 1967 with elections for city posts in Bangkok. In 1968 a new constitution was put into effect, and elections for positions in the nation's legislature were held during the next year. But a weakening economy and the presence of Communist forces on Thailand's borders—especially in Laos—prompted Thanom to suspend the constitution in 1971 and to set up another military government.

Thanom introduced a new constitution in 1972, but many university students were not satisfied with the proposed structure of government. In early 1973 the students demonstrated for democratic reforms. The protests grew stronger over the months, until mid-October, when 250,000 people gathered in Bangkok. The government troops fired on the assembled protesters and killed about 75 of them. King Bhumibol intervened during the crisis and negotiated with Thanom. As a result, Thanom and his top officials resigned their posts and left the country secretly.

Another constitution was enacted in 1974, and new elections in 1975 brought in a civilian government. The administration, however, struggled to maintain unity among its own leaders. When Thanom returned to Thailand in 1976 to attend his father's funeral, tensions in the country increased, and students demonstrated against his presence. Later in the year, Admiral Sa-Ngad Choloryu led a coup against the civilian government, voided the constitution, and put Thailand under martial law.

After yet another constitution was drafted in 1978, Thai administrations continued to revolve in and out of power. In 1980, however, General Prem Tinsulanonda became prime minister, and his government survived coup attempts in 1981, 1983, and 1985. The king steadily backed Prem, and an increase in the prime minister's supporters in the legislature strengthened his control of the government.

Recent Events

In the 1980s Thai leaders worked both to limit the influence of Communist revolutionaries within Thailand and to prevent bordering Communist countries from expanding into the nation's territory. Prem Tinsulanonda organized a campaign against Communist guerrillas operating in Thailand, and in 1986 he reported that all but several hundred of them had been captured or killed.

In July 1988, popular elections were held for the national assembly. The newly elected legislative body chose former army general Chatichai Choonhavan to be the new prime minister. The transfer of power from Prem to the new leader was accomplished smoothly.

Warfare in the region, mainly between Vietnam and Kampuchea, has brought a flood of refugees to Thailand. Fleeing conflict in their homelands, these people cluster in camps inside the Thai border.

With so many refugees in the country already, the Thai have begun to regulate the number of new arrivals. Thai patrols monitor the Laotian and Kampuchean borders, and the Thai navy has begun turning away Vietnamese refugees who approach Thailand by sea. Thai officials have asked other nations in the region and Western countries to take in some of the growing refugee population. In 1988 the Vietnamese began the first stage of troop withdrawal from Kampuchea. The Thai

Having completed a dangerous sea journey to Thailand in open boats, these Vietnamese people unload their belongings at a refugee camp. The Thai government has urged Western nations to help relocate the large number of refugees that pour into Thailand from neighboring Southeast Asian countries.

government hopes that the number of refugees will decline as the level of conflict in the region decreases.

Government

The constitution established in 1978 is the fourteenth put into effect since Thailand became a constitutional monarchy in 1932. Under this form of government, a king serves as head of state. His duty is to give consent to governmental appointments that the prime minister and the national assembly present to him. The assembly chooses the prime minister, who then selects a council to run the departments of the government.

The national assembly contains the house of representatives, whose members are publicly elected and serve for four years. The assembly also has a senate, whose delegates the prime minister names to six-year terms.

The supreme court, which has six members, is the highest court in Thailand. The nation also has a court of appeals and courts of first instance. Local courts administer laws concerning marriage, inheritance, and other family matters. In the southern region—where many Thai are Malay Muslims (followers of the Islamic religion)—local qadi (Islamic judges) administer sharia (law based on the Koran, Islam's holy book).

Thailand is divided into 73 provinces, each of which is ruled by a governor. Groups of villages organize themselves into associations called *tambols*. One person, known as the *kamnan*, is elected from among the village leaders to represent the tambol to the provincial governor and to help solve regional disputes.

Photo by Amandus Schneider

The ornate buildings and spacious halls of the Royal Palace in Bangkok are the diplomatic headquarters for meetings between Thai government leaders and foreign dignitaries. The grounds also contain the king's ceremonial residence.

Among the Lisu—a hill people of northern Thailand—very young children often carry babies on their backs. The Lisu live at elevations over 5,000 feet above sea level and have depended on opium poppies as their most important crop. In the 1980s, large numbers of visiting tourists have disrupted the hill peoples' traditional way of life.

Photo by Mirjam van der Heyden and Charlie Rabelink

3) The People

In 1988, 54.7 million people lived in Thailand. The nation's annual growth rate of 2.1 percent in 1988 has slowed significantly from 3.1 percent—the rate that the nation registered in 1960.

Thailand is primarily a rural nation, with 83 percent of its population living on farms or in villages. Since 1960, however, the flow of people to the cities, and especially to Bangkok, has steadily increased because of opportunities for higher-paying jobs and better education.

Rural settlement patterns have also changed in recent years. As farmland has become scarce, many Thai have moved to the less populated northern region of the country to begin new farms on the mountainsides and in the river valleys.

Ethnic Groups

All citizens of Thailand, no matter what their ethnic ties, are called Thai. But a group known as ethnic Thai make up 85 percent of the Thai population. The ethnic Thai fall into four subgroups that are determined by geographic location within the country and by distinctive language variations.

Chinese settlers have inhabited Thailand for many centuries and make up 8 percent of the population in the late 1980s. Until the early twentieth century, most Chinese immigrants were unmarried men who eventually married local women. Entire Chinese families began to immigrate to Thailand in the 1920s, but the newcomers were not as easily absorbed into Thai communities as Chinese-Thai couples were. Later in the twentieth century, Chinese workers competed with Thai laborers for jobs. This situation, coupled with the deep antagonism that many Thai had toward the People's Republic of China and its Communist system, has prompted anti-Chinese sentiments among some Thai.

These boys are members of the Thai ethnic group, to which four out of five Thai citizens belong. The Thai people originated in China and began migrating from there about 1,300 years ago.

Photo by Jane L. Anglin

Courtesy of Robert E. Olson

These children of Indian descent live in Chiang Mai. They belong to one of the small ethnic communities whose ancestors have come to Thailand from many parts of Asia.

Photo by Daniel H. Condit

These two young members of the Karen ethnic group are wearing clothing that indicates their unmarried status. Most villages of Karen people are located in the mountains along the Thai border with Burma.

About 3 percent of Thailand's population is made up of Malays who live in the southern peninsular region, near the Malaysian border. Almost all Malay Thai are members of Islam—a religion founded in Arabia during the seventh century. Malay Thai work predominantly as rubber tree planters, farmers, and fishermen.

Many members of the Mon and the Khmer ethnic groups have blended with the larger Thai community. Since the mid-1970s, many Khmer have come to Thailand as refugees from warfare in Kampuchea. Camps on the Thai-Kampuchean border contain more than 300,000 Khmer.

In northern Thailand and along the western border are many small ethnic groups identified as hill peoples. One of the largest of these is the Hmong. Members of this group migrated into Thailand at the beginning of the nineteenth century from Laos and China. They live in villages in the mountains and raise rice, maize (corn), and opium poppies. Because poppies are the source of opium, which is an illegal drug, Thai authorities have destroyed many poppy harvests and encourage the Hmong and other poppy growers to grow other crops.

Religion

More than 95 percent of the people in Thailand are Buddhists. This religion follows the teachings of Gautama Buddha (Buddha means "Enlightened One"), who founded Buddhism in India in the sixth century B.C. Buddha's ideas included the notion of a constant cycle of death and rebirth called reincarnation. He also believed that freedom from suffering could be achieved through detachment from material things.

Buddhism in Thailand has its roots in a Buddhist sect named Theravada, meaning "Way of the Elders," which Sri Lankan

Photo by Bernice K. Condit

Buddhist monks carry alms bowls (begging dishes) on a street in Chiang Mai. As part of Buddhist tradition, the monks ask local families to provide their daily food.

monks introduced to the region. This branch of Buddhism focuses particularly on the monastic way of life and on the Buddhist scriptures known as the Tripitika. Forty percent of the men in Thailand over the age of 20 become monks for a period of time—from a few days to several months. As monks, they beg for food, study Buddhist writings, and pray each day.

Many Chinese Thai follow Confucianism, which is a philosophical approach to life that stresses the development of moral character. Begun in the sixth century B.C. by a Chinese scholar named Confucius, this system of thought emphasizes order in family and civic life, as well as respect for one's ancestors.

The Malay Thai are predominantly Muslims—followers of Islam. Muslims pray five times per day, fast during the holy month of Ramadan, and, if possible, make a pilgrimage to the holy city of Mecca in

Faithful Buddhists pray in the Wat Phra Keo, which holds the revered emerald statue of Buddha.

Young students of Buddhism sit at the base of a bo tree, like the one under which Buddha meditated. In recent years, the Thai custom that all young men become monks, at least for a short time, has declined.

40

Photo by Drs. A. A. M. van der Heyden, Naarden, the Netherlands

Jeweled prangs are architectural features of the Wat Phra Keo in Bangkok. Each prang honors Buddha or a Buddhist holy person.

Saudi Arabia on at least one occasion in their lifetime.

The ethnic groups that live in the mountains—as well as many people who follow Buddhism, Confucianism, and Islam—practice a number of local religious beliefs. They ask spirits for aid and protection by offering incense, flowers, and food. They leave these items in miniature houses built for the spirits in cities, towns, and villages.

Language

The Thai language belongs to the Chinese-Tibetan family of languages, which includes Chinese, Burmese, and Tibetan. Composed mainly of one-syllable words—each of which has several different translations—Thai speech depends on the tone of the spoken word to distinguish one meaning from another. The five tones—rising or falling, high or low, or an even tone—indicate different meanings for a single

Photo by Jane L. Anglin

To encourage local spirits to bring them good luck, Thai people often place floral offerings in shrines on the grounds of public buildings.

Photo by Josh Kohnstamm

The Pepsi symbol, inscribed with Thai lettering, suggests the high degree of contact Thailand has with Western customs and products.

41

word. The position in which the word appears in a sentence also helps to determine its sense.

The Thai writing system has 44 consonants and 32 vowels, with tone markings placed above the letters. The script that King Rama Khamhaeng developed in the fourteenth century was based on a pattern of Khmer characters. Thai letters are curved and flowing, and they are written left to right without punctuation.

The four dialects of the Thai language correspond to the country's four main geographical regions: central, northern, northeastern (Khorat Plateau), and southern. Vocabulary is basically the same for all of the dialects, but the tonal patterns are different. After becoming familiar with tones of another region, speakers of different dialects can communicate with each other.

Central Thai is the official language of the nation, and it is used in schools, in newspapers, and in television and radio broadcasts. Malay Thai, many of whom are not fluent in Thai, speak the Malay language. Most Chinese Thai speak the official national language as well as Chinese. Members of the various hill groups speak one of several non-Thai languages and usually know only enough Thai to function as traders.

Education

In the early twentieth century, Thai leaders began to plan a new educational system. In 1921 the king decreed a policy of free education for all Thai children. In the 1940s and 1950s, enough schools were built and enough teachers were trained for the nation's children to be instructed on a

These girls attend primary school in Kamphaeng Phet, a small city about 220 miles north of Bangkok. Education is compulsory through the sixth grade in Thailand.

large scale. In the 1980s, 20 percent of the national budget was spent on education.

Attendance at primary school is compulsory for all Thai between the ages of 7 and 14. Through a combination of public and private schools, 97 percent of the eligible population is enrolled at the primary level. About 30 percent go on to the secondary stage, which lasts for six years. Thailand's literacy rate of 92 percent for men and 84 percent for women is above average for Southeast Asian countries.

Of Thailand's 17 universities, several are located in Bangkok—including Chulalongkorn University, founded in 1917, and Thammasat University, opened in 1934. The government has established several universities in locations other than Bangkok to make higher education more widely available. For example, Chiang Mai University opened in 1964 in the northern Thai city from which it takes its name. Thailand also has 36 colleges of education and more than 200 vocational and agricultural institutions.

Photo by Bernice K. Condit

A woman of the Karen hill people in northern Thailand fills a bamboo container with river water. Unsafe drinking water has caused many health problems in Thailand, particularly in the south.

Health

Health care in Thailand has steadily improved during the second half of the twentieth century. Widespread antidisease programs begun in the 1960s have limited the occurrence of cholera, tetanus, tuberculosis, and smallpox. Chemical sprays have reduced the malaria-carrying mosquito population, and drugs to treat the disease are widely used. The government has improved sanitation facilities and has increased the availability of safe drinking water. As a result, intestinal diseases, which can be fatal, occur less frequently.

By the 1980s, Thai medical schools had trained enough health-care professionals to replace the many Western medical personnel who had worked in the nation during the twentieth century. The government has sponsored the construction of over 400 hospitals and more than 2,000 clinics throughout the country. High-quality health care is now available to those who live outside Bangkok, previously the nation's only medical center.

In 1974 the government's Public Welfare Department set up family-planning centers in every region of the nation. These centers not only provide education about family planning—which has resulted in a lower population growth rate—but also inform the public about nutrition, sanitation, and disease prevention. These and other measures have helped increase Thai life expectancy from 51 years in 1960 to 64 years in 1988. The infant mortality rate has also improved because of better health care. In 1988, 52 infants died out of every 1,000 live births—a significantly lower rate than the 72 deaths per 1,000 that is the average in Southeast Asia.

One of the most serious health problems in Bangkok and in the country's other tourist centers is related to prostitution.

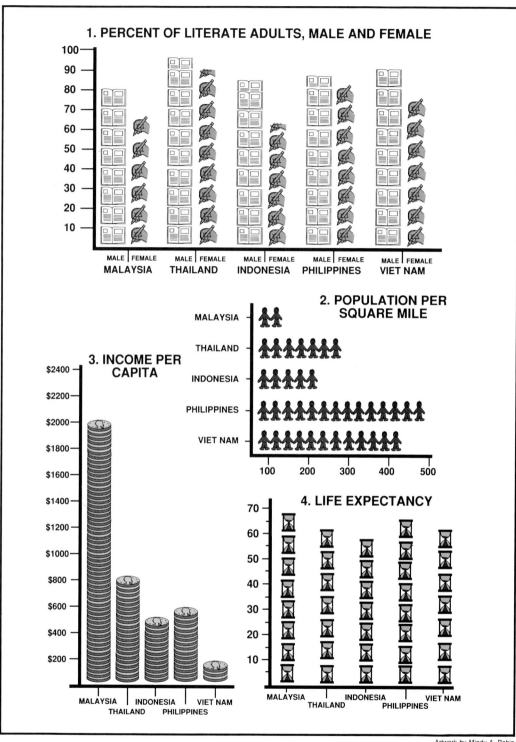

Depicted in this chart are factors relating to the standard of living in five countries in southeastern Asia. Information taken from "1987 World Population Data Sheet," "The World's Women: A Profile," and "Children of the World" compiled by the Population Reference Bureau, Washington, D.C.

Photo by Amandus Schneider

Over 250,000 Thai in Bangkok accept money in exchange for sexual encounters, a practice that increases the threat of contracting acquired immune deficiency syndrome (AIDS). Testing for and recording the incidences of AIDS is difficult when so many people—both local and foreign—are involved in prostitution.

The Arts

Dance and drama are highly developed arts in Thailand. Folk epics—especially an Indian tale of the god Rama, called the *Ramakien* in Thai—are enacted by dancers with precise and graceful movements. *Khon* is the most formal style of dance. Performers wear masks and elaborate, gem-covered costumes. The movements of the dancers express parts of the story. Khon dancers do not speak but are accompanied by a chorus that communicates the necessary dialogue.

Lakon is a less formal kind of Thai dance. Lakon performers do not wear masks, and they speak the lines of the story. Many Thai consider lakon to be the most graceful of the nation's dance forms, and female dancers most often perform the movements.

45

Thai shadow plays, known as *nang*, are enacted by artists who use the cut-out shapes of characters made from animal skins to tell a story. By moving the shapes in front of a lamp, nang players cast shadows onto a large screen for the audience to see. *Hun* is Thai puppet theater, and the puppets are worked by players who sit below a specially built stage.

Musicians accompany khon, lakon, nang, hun, and other forms of dance and theater. Musical ensembles usually have 5 to 10 members who play either wind or percussion instruments. Traditional Thai music is unwritten but has survived because each generation of musicians has passed it on to the next.

Thai literature has its roots in ancient folk tales. For example, the fifteenth-century story *Phra Law* tells of the rivalry between two northern clans and the war that erupts between them. Traditional Thai writing became more religious as Buddhist influence grew. Thai stories were most often told in verse, but modern Thai literature has largely abandoned poetic form. Thai writers in the twentieth century express themselves in novels, short stories, and essays.

Thailand's tradition of handicrafts is widely varied. In the northern portion of the country, silversmiths make elegant silver bowls, boxes, and trays. Other craftspeople in the region produce brightly painted umbrellas. The Khorat Plateau is the center of the silk industry, where each worker daily weaves two to three yards of silk cloth on handlooms.

Photo by Andrew E. Beswick

The fingernail dance originated in northern Thailand. At one time, women's long fingernails were symbols of wealth and beauty. The bronze and gold fingernails worn by dancers enhance their graceful hand movements.

This Thai instrument, a type of flute, is made of pierced bamboo and sounds like a Scottish bagpipe.

Independent Picture Service

A temple mural depicts scenes from the *Ramakien* – the Thai version of a famous Indian epic tale of royal exile, brave deeds, and religious and marital devotion.

Buddhist monks often help with community projects. Here, several monks show villagers how to weave mats.

Photo by Amandus Schneider

Mythological Garudas adorn some Thai temples. Half bird and half human, the fierce-looking Garuda is the creature on which the Hindu god Vishnu rides.

Photo by Jane L. Anglin

A woman weaves cloth—an important Thai artform and export—on a wooden handloom.

Courtesy of Edith Lurvey

Thai artisans have made fine porcelain since the late thirteenth century, when Rama Khamhaeng invited Chinese craftspeople to the region to teach pottery skills to local people.

Wood carvings, often made from teak, are crafted in many regions of the country. Porcelain making—an art learned from the Chinese—and the production of lacquer ware are also widespread Thai handicrafts.

Sports

People in several Southeast Asian countries engage in the sport of kite-flying. Stretched tightly on bamboo frames, kites in Thailand are made of beautifully illustrated paper. Teams of up to 10 people fly large five-pointed *chula* kites. Smaller, more managable *pakpao* kites confront the large kites in aerial fights, and each kite tries to make the others fall to the ground.

Takraw is another sport played throughout much of Southeast Asia. A ball woven from tough palm stems (rattan) is hit back and forth over a net or into a hoop. Players keep the ball in the air by bouncing it off

Before a Thai boxing match begins, the participants pray to sacred spirits. The main weapons of the boxers are their feet, but they also use their elbows, shoulders, and knees to defeat their opponents.

their heads or feet, but they may not use their hands. A team scores points when it puts the ball through the hoop or when the other team allows the ball to hit the ground.

Unique to Thailand is a ritualized form of boxing. Participants ask the aid of spirits by prayerfully bowing and kneeling in the ring before the match begins. Boxers use their bare feet, elbows, knees, and gloved hands as they fight each other.

Food

Thai food is often spicy with contrasting sweet, sour, and salty tastes. From the Chinese, Thai cooks learned how to prepare small, cut-up pieces of food by stirring them in a very hot, lightly oiled pan —a technique known as stir-frying. Thai cuisine also makes use of curry, a combination of spices that originated in India. Coconut milk sometimes flavors Thai food and mellows the spicier dishes.

The Thai eat rice with almost every meal. People in the Khorat Plateau prefer the short-grained, sticky variety of rice

Kite makers take great care with the size, shape, and decoration of their designs, which are put on heavy paper and stretched over bamboo frames.

that grows in the area, but most of the people of Thailand eat the more common long-grained rice.

Seafood from the Gulf of Thailand and fish from the nation's rivers make up a large part of the Thai diet. Mussels, crabs, lobsters, scallops, shrimp, and squid are often served at meals, and the many varieties of fish are eaten in fresh, salted, dried, and pickled forms.

Bananas, pineapples, papayas, and mangoes are among the most popular fruits in Thailand. Rambutans (red, oval-shaped fruit), mangosteens (reddish brown fruit with a flavor similar to a mixture of peach and pineapple), and shaddocks (an Asian version of grapefruit) are native to the region.

Noodles made from rice, eggs, or mung beans are a regular part of Thai meals. Fried rice, curried chicken, and salads made with vegetables and small amounts of beef are some favorite dishes. At most of their meals, the Thai use a sauce called *nam pla prig,* which is made of fish sauce, garlic, red peppers, and lemon juice.

Meals in Thailand are often artistically arranged, especially during national festivals such as the king's birthday or New Year's Day. During traditional celebrations, the low tables in Thai dining areas are arrayed with fruits and vegetables cut into decorative shapes. Diners commonly sit on the floor, serve themselves from small bowls arranged around their plates, and eat with forks and spoons.

Photo by Drs. A. A. M. van der Heyden, Naarden, the Netherlands

Vendors sell locally grown produce at an early morning market in Bangkok. The Thai diet relies heavily on fruits and vegetables.

Women set rice plants into a flooded paddy (rice field) in Thailand's central plain. Seedlings grow in several inches of water until the grain begins to ripen, then the water is drained. Nearly all villagers, including children, participate in rice cultivation.

4) The Economy

In the 1980s, the Thai economy began to shift its emphasis from agriculture to industry. Although still predominantly a farming nation—over 60 percent of its people work in agriculture—Thailand relies much less on exports of farm products for income than it did at one time. In the late 1970s, Thai crops accounted for about 70 percent of the nation's export income, but by the late 1980s only 40 percent of the export revenue came from agriculture. Agricultural workers earn only a fraction of what urban laborers receive.

Not only has the agricultural portion of the economy declined in overall importance, but Thai farmers also have changed their focus significantly. Rice was once the nation's only major export crop. But low prices for rice on the world market and increased production of rice by other countries have caused Thai farmers to grow a variety of crops.

Textiles, electronics, and automobile manufacturing are some of Thailand's fastest growing new industries. Low taxes and a large, educated work force encourage Thai and foreign business leaders to invest billions of dollars each year in the Thai economy.

Agriculture

Thai farmers cultivate about 40 percent of the nation's land area, and three out of four farmers own the land that they work. An average farm is about 10 acres in size and is divided into small plots.

Thailand's central plain is known as the rice bowl area, because farmers in this region grow most of the rice that is exported. The Chao Phraya River and its tributaries overflow during the southwest monsoon season, and floodwaters cover the paddies (rice fields), which are divided by earthen barriers. Water buffalo are used to plow the flooded fields, and in July workers transplant bunches of four or five rice seedlings from nursery beds into the paddies.

Klongs help control the floodwaters on the central plain. When the rains diminish, the canals carry water from reservoirs

Courtesy of United Nations

This irrigation canal on a farm in northeastern Thailand is part of a development project along the Mekong River that the United Nations started in 1966. Irrigation helps to control weeds that can crowd rice seedlings.

By leading them around in circles, these farmers get their water buffalo to trample bundles of dried rice. This activity breaks the grain away from the stalks.

Young farm workers beat piled rice to separate husks from kernels. This hulling method leaves the nutritious bran coating of each kernel intact. The resulting rice is brown, not white.

HASHISH AND OPIATE PRODUCTION AND SUPPLY, 1986

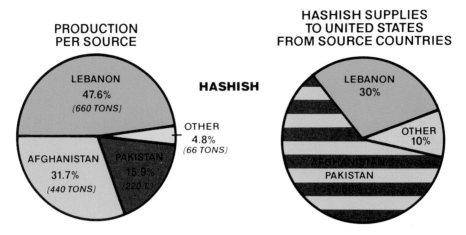

PRODUCTION PER SOURCE

HASHISH

LEBANON
47.6%
(660 TONS)

OTHER
4.8%
(66 TONS)

AFGHANISTAN
31.7%
(440 TONS)

PAKISTAN
15.9%
(220 T.)

HASHISH SUPPLIES TO UNITED STATES FROM SOURCE COUNTRIES

LEBANON
30%

OTHER
10%

AFGHANISTAN/
PAKISTAN
60%

(India and Nepal consume and export domestically grown hashish, but to what extent is unknown. Over six tons of hashish originating in India were seized in North America in 1986.)

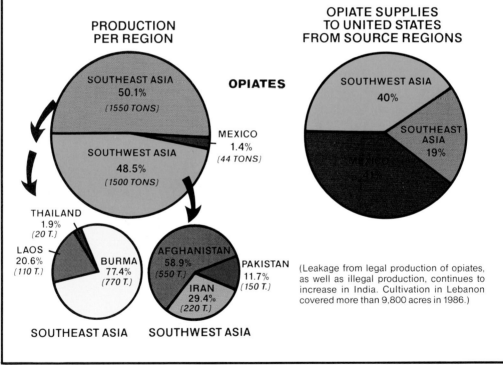

PRODUCTION PER REGION

OPIATES

SOUTHEAST ASIA
50.1%
(1550 TONS)

MEXICO
1.4%
(44 TONS)

SOUTHWEST ASIA
48.5%
(1500 TONS)

THAILAND
1.9%
(20 T.)

LAOS
20.6%
(110 T.)

BURMA
77.4%
(770 T.)

AFGHANISTAN
58.9%
(550 T.)

PAKISTAN
11.7%
(150 T.)

IRAN
29.4%
(220 T.)

SOUTHEAST ASIA   SOUTHWEST ASIA

OPIATE SUPPLIES TO UNITED STATES FROM SOURCE REGIONS

SOUTHWEST ASIA
40%

SOUTHEAST
ASIA
19%

MEXICO
41%

(Leakage from legal production of opiates, as well as illegal production, continues to increase in India. Cultivation in Lebanon covered more than 9,800 acres in 1986.)

Artwork by Elizabeth Pilon

These pie charts depict data about both the production and U.S. supplies of two kinds of drugs. Hashish is a substance taken from the *Cannabis sativa* plant, which also is a source of marijuana. Opiates are drugs that come from opium poppies *(Papaver somniferum)*, mostly in the refined forms of opium and heroin. The production pies *(left)* cover the percentages estimated to be manufactured by each country or region. The pies depicting U.S. supplies *(right)* illustrate only percentages that arrive in the United States. They do not include amounts used within source countries or regions, nor do they illustrate percentages that go to other parts of the world. Data taken from the *NNICC Report, 1985–1986* compiled by the U.S. Drug Enforcement Administration, Washington, D.C.

formed by the Phumiphon, Sirikit, and other dams on the Chao Phraya. In November the winds of the northeast monsoon dry out the paddies, and the farmers harvest the rice.

Maize and sugarcane are major crops that grow on the edges of the central plain. Situated at a slightly higher elevation, these areas are not likely to flood during the rainy season. In other parts of the country, farmers grow rice as a food crop for the local population rather than for export. In the mountains, rice, maize, and vegetables are the main agricultural products.

Farmers from the hill groups often cut and burn the natural mountainside vegetation to make new fields for their crops. After a few years of planting, the soil is no longer fertile, and the farmers move to new territory to begin the cycle of burning natural vegetation and planting crops again. This practice causes soil erosion, which is severely damaging the environment of northern Thailand.

In some areas, hill people grow opium poppies as a cash (money-earning) crop. The territory on the borders of Burma, Laos, and Thailand—where the poppies are widely cultivated—is known as the Golden Triangle. Because of pressure from the Thai government to stop this illegal activity, the amount of opium produced from local poppy crops fell from 35 tons in 1983 to about 20 tons in 1986.

The Khorat Plateau is less fertile than the rest of the country, but rice can be planted in paddies that are situated near rivers. The farmers in this region grow a short-grained type of rice. Since the 1960s cassava (a starchy root) has also become one of the region's export crops.

In the southern peninsula, farmers cultivate rice, pineapples, bananas, and cotton. Thai farmers also raise flowers, especially orchids, for local and export markets. Livestock on Thai farms include water buffalo and cattle, both of which are used as draft (load-pulling) animals. Farmers raise pigs,

Photo by Daniel H. Condit

Newly cut stalks of green bananas are ready to be collected on Thailand's southern peninsula.

Photo by Josh Kohnstamm

Fresh vegetables and fruit displayed at a Bangkok market indicate the variety of produce raised in Thailand, one of the world's largest food exporters.

Lumber industry workers float teak logs along a chute for processing at a sawmill. Because teak is a durable and valuable wood, each log is cut carefully to avoid waste. Teak is used primarily for furniture and shipbuilding.

chickens, and ducks as well, mostly for food.

Forestry and Fishing

Thailand's forests are among the nation's most valuable resources. Evergreen and deciduous (leaf-shedding) trees provide fuel for cooking and heating as well as the raw material for furniture, housing, shipbuilding, and carved artworks. The govern-

ment regulates the forests and attempts to protect them from inefficient harvesting. Thailand also sponsors a reforestation program to renew this natural resource.

Teak trees grow in the northern mountain region and are Thailand's most precious timber. Teak trees require from 80 to 150 years to mature. The wood from these trees is strong, durable, and water-resistant. Foresters harvest teak by cutting away a ring of its bark and drilling a

Elephants are an essential part of the logging industry of northern Thailand, where they carry cut timber over rough ground. An elephant can transport a log weighing about 4,000 pounds.

Courtesy of FAO

hole into the center of the tree. After the trees are killed in this way, they are left standing for two years to season and dry the wood. Other valuable Thai trees include mahogany, ebony, rosewood, and rattan palm.

Farmers in the southern peninsula grow rubber trees on small plots of land. The sap from the trees—called latex—is the raw material for making rubber. Planted at the beginning of the twentieth century, many rubber trees in Thailand are past their latex-producing prime. In the 1970s and 1980s, a new high-yielding variety of tree was planted to replace many of the older trees.

Fish and other seafood supply a major portion of the people's protein needs. Recent improvements—such as modernized boats—in the country's deep-sea fishing fleet have led to a large increase in the salt-water catch, which averaged two million

Thai farmers use nets, traps, and poles to catch fish and shellfish from local ponds and canals.

Courtesy of John Seo, FFH

tons in the late 1980s. The number of fishing boats also increased from a few thousand to 20,000 in recent years. The shrimp catch has been particularly large, and fresh and frozen shrimp have become a leading Thai export.

Freshwater species are abundant in Thailand's rivers, lakes, klongs, ponds, and rice paddies. Many rural Thai angle in these waterways, and local markets stock a wide variety of freshwater fish.

Industry and Mining

Many of Thailand's industries are located in and around Bangkok—the nation's major import and export center. Companies from Japan, the United States, and other nations have invested in Thailand's growing industrial economy. The country's new manufacturing sector produces electronic circuits, parts for telephones, and computer hardware.

The textile industry has been an important part of Thailand's economy since the early twentieth century. Silk and cotton

Courtesy of FFH

Basket weaving is one of Thailand's oldest crafts. This artisan makes items that will hold produce and other goods.

Photo by Jane L. Anglin

A young woman paints flowers on parasols (sunshades) made from paper and bamboo.

Thailand's industrial sector has grown in recent years, offering job opportunities to skilled Thai workers. Many products that were once imported are now manufactured locally.

are woven in many urban mills. Villagers also produce cloth as a way to earn money while working at home. In the 1980s, Thai designers began to produce fashion clothing as well as textiles. Over one-fourth of all goods made in Thailand are textiles.

Thai manufacturers have developed a large food-processing industry, and the nation has become the largest producer of canned pineapple and canned tuna in the world. Other areas of industrial growth include cement plants and sugarcane refineries. By expanding their facilities, owners have almost doubled their production capacity since 1950.

Thai workers in the southern peninsula mine large amounts of tin ore, and Thailand is consistently among the world's top three suppliers of tin. In addition, the nation mines bauxite (from which aluminum is made), iron ore, and manganese. Precious gemstones, especially sapphires, are another important product of the country's mining sector.

One of Thailand's economic difficulties has been its reliance on petroleum imports,

Workers have prepared a barge fitted with a crane to lift a section of an offshore drilling rig that is being constructed in the Gulf of Thailand. The gulf contains deposits of natural gas.

but discoveries of natural gas in the Gulf of Thailand have eased this problem. By 1985 the country had developed four gas fields in the gulf, and much of the gas was used to fuel electricity-generating plants near Bangkok. In the mid-1980s, exploratory drilling crews discovered petroleum in the western part of the country. By the late 1980s, workers had begun to build a new petrochemical plant near Rayong to process the oil from the newly discovered reserves.

Transportation

The transportation network in Thailand consists of roads, railways, waterways, and domestic and international air routes. Over 27,000 miles of roadway are paved with asphalt, and another 70,000 miles are secondary gravel roads. Buses and cars travel between large population centers, and, in the cities, rickshas (two-wheeled vehicles pulled by one person), three-wheeled motorized carts, and motorcycles also provide transportation. Because of

As the contents of this university parking lot indicate, motorcycles are a popular mode of transportation in Thai cities.

Photo by Jane L. Anglin

Small sampans (flat-bottomed boats) laden with goods make their way up a klong in Bangkok. Canals remain important transportation routes in many parts of the country.

Courtesy of Minneapolis Public Library and Information Center

60

As children scramble out of the way, large trucks roll down an unpaved road enroute to an oil exploration site.

the rapid population growth in Bangkok, traffic is congested and slow-moving.

The State Railway of Thailand oversees 2,800 miles of railroad track. Four main routes radiate from Bangkok to the four main geographical districts. The rail lines run to Chiang Mai in the north, to Arayaprathet in the east, to Ubon Ratchathani City on the Khorat Plateau, and to the Malaysian border in the south.

The rivers and klongs of the central plain provide an extensive transportation route for people and agricultural goods on the way to Bangkok. As Thailand's central city, Bangkok is also a crowded port that receives goods from abroad and sends Thai materials and finished products overseas.

Thai Airways International and other airlines fly from Thailand's four international airports, which are located in Bangkok, Chiang Mai, Phuket, and Hat Yai.

Thai Airways Company is the nation's domestic airline and connects smaller towns to one another and to Bangkok.

Tourism

Tourism is one of Thailand's fastest-growing industries and employs over one million people. Tourists from many parts of the world—including Japan, the Middle East, the United States, and Europe—come to Thailand to visit the nation's resorts, beaches, and palaces. Pattaya, southwest of Bangkok, and Phuket are two of the largest resort areas. The ruins of palaces and temples at Ayutthaya and Sukhothai in central Thailand are among the sites that travelers often stop to see.

With its markets, nightlife, historical landmarks, and varied cultural events, Bangkok attracts the largest number of

Tourists stroll through the Royal Palace, one of the architectural highlights of Bangkok. Tourism is an important and growing source of income for Thailand.

Gold-covered tiles, precious stones, and ornate statues appear throughout the grounds of the Royal Palace.

tourists. Almost all visitors to Thailand spend time at the Grand Palace, which is in the oldest part of Bangkok. In the late eighteenth century, King Chakkri built the first royal residence on the site. Since then, several kings have constructed their own residences, as well as adding religious and civic buildings. The palace grounds contain several wats—Buddhist religious compounds made up of temples, monastery buildings, and meditation halls.

The Future

Because Thailand broadened its financial base in the 1980s, the Thai people are optimistic about their country's economic future. International corporations are attracted to Thailand because of its skilled and inexpensive work force and because of the tax incentives offered by the Thai government.

Bangkok has gained most of the benefit from the nation's economic growth. But it has also suffered the difficulties that come with rapid development—overcrowded residential areas, traffic congestion, sanitation and pollution difficulties, and increased crime. In contrast to the expanded opportunities enjoyed by residents of Bangkok, rural workers have become impatient with wages that are one-eighth of what urban workers receive. Government economic planners are searching for a way to balance this inequality.

On the international level, Thailand is concerned about the political problems of its Southeast Asian neighbors. In 1988 the government of Burma collapsed and struggled to find new leadership, and the war in Kampuchea continued. More stable than nearby countries, Thailand still has a history of frequent coups and coup-attempts that makes its citizens anxious about the government's ability to last. Thai leaders hope that continued economic growth will both protect the nation from other upheavals in the region and foster political growth within the country.

Photo by Amandus Schneider

Delicate gold carvings form the bow of a royal barge.

Photo by Reuters/Bettmann Newsphotos

Prime Minister Chatichai Choonhavan prayed at the Government House in Bangkok before taking over the job from his predecessor, Prem Tinsulanonda, in August 1988.

Index